Get Ready for Pre-K

Jumbo Workbook

This workbook belongs to

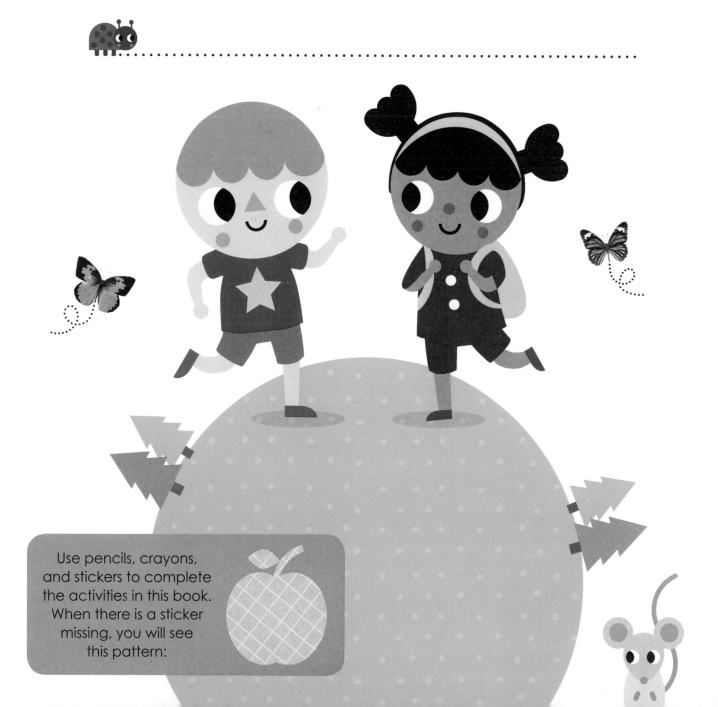

Use pencils, crayons, and stickers to complete the activities in this book. When there is a sticker missing, you will see this pattern:

Dear Parents,

Welcome to the *Jumbo Get Ready for Pre-K Workbook!*

Here are some tips to help ensure that your child gets the most from this book.

★ Look at the pages with your child, ensuring he or she knows what to do before starting.

★ Plan short, regular sessions, doing only one or two pages at a time.

★ Praise your child's efforts and improvements.

★ Encourage your child to assess his or her own efforts in a positive way. For example, say: "You've drawn some great triangles there. Which one do you think you did best?"

★ Make the learning sessions positive experiences. Give prompts where they might help. If a section is too hard for your child, leave those pages until he or she is ready for them.

★ Relate the learning to things in your child's world. For example, if your child is working on a page about the color red, ask him or her to find some red things in your home.

★ There are stickers to use throughout the book. They help build your child's hand-eye coordination and observation skills. Encourage your child to place the stickers on each page before starting the other activities.

Together, the activities in the workbook help build a solid understanding of early learning concepts to ensure your child is ready for pre-k or preschool.

We wish your child hours of enjoyment with this fun workbook!

Scholastic Early Learning

Contents

Party fun

Trace the strings on the balloons.
Start at the big red dot.

Smart stripes

Trace the stripes on the boy's T-shirt.

Picture gallery

Trace the picture frames.

Rainbow kites

Trace the kites.

Starfish

Trace the starfish.

Birthday gift

Trace the gift.

The horse's stable

Trace the stable door.

Flower fun

Trace the petals on the flower.

Googly glasses

Trace the girl's toy glasses.

Lollipop!

Trace the spiral in the lollipop.

Wiggly snakes

Trace the snakes.

Lots of legs

Trace the octopus's legs.

Beautiful beads

Trace the pretty beads on the necklace.

Tasty watermelon

Trace the watermelon slices.

Cute cat

Trace the cat.

A cool car

Trace the car.

Lots of dots

Trace the ladybug.

Blast off!

Trace the rocket.

Five little ducks

Help the ducks reach the other side of the pond.

Start→

Finish

22

Bunny's burrow

Help the rabbit find its way back to its bunnies.

Chirping chicks

Help the hen find her chicks.

Start

Finish

Car race

Help the race car reach the finish line.

Start →

→ Finish

Fun on the farm

Help the farmer find his tractor.

Start ←

Finish ←

Web wander

Help the spider find its way through the web.

Start

Finish

Pig puzzle

Help the pig return to its pigsty.

Start ←

Finish ←

Monkey business

Help the monkey reach the bananas.

Start →

Finish

Cheese, please!

Help the mouse find the cheese.

Start→

→Finish

Teddy bear's picnic

Help the teddy bear find the picnic.

Start

Finish

Fishy friends

Help the fish swim to its friend.

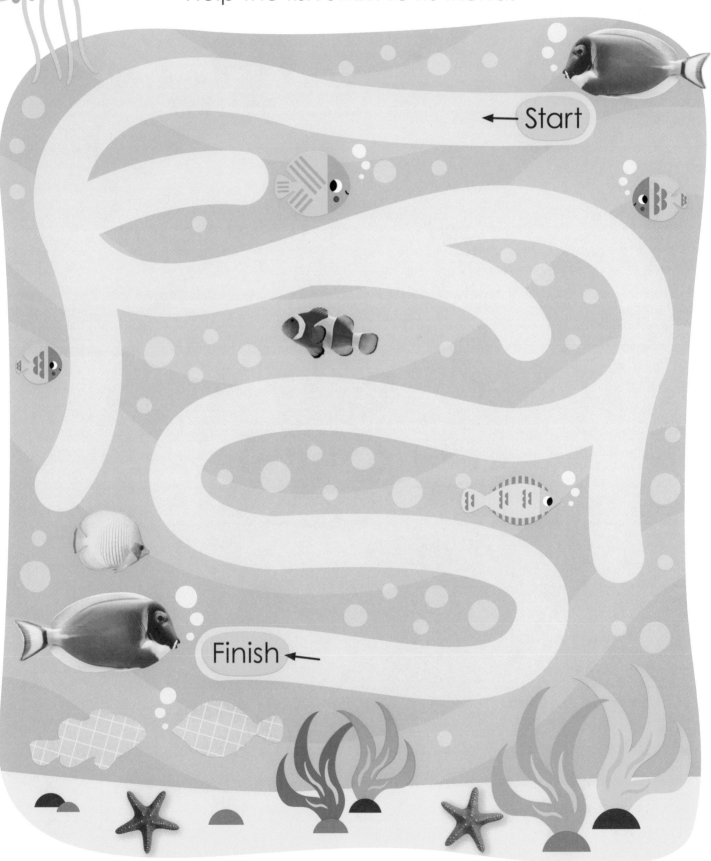

Start

Finish

Playground games

Help the children find the playground.

Start →

→ Finish

Home time

Help the family bike home.

Start

Finish

Puppy love

Help the dog find its puppy.

Start →

Finish

Story time

Help the teacher find the storybook.

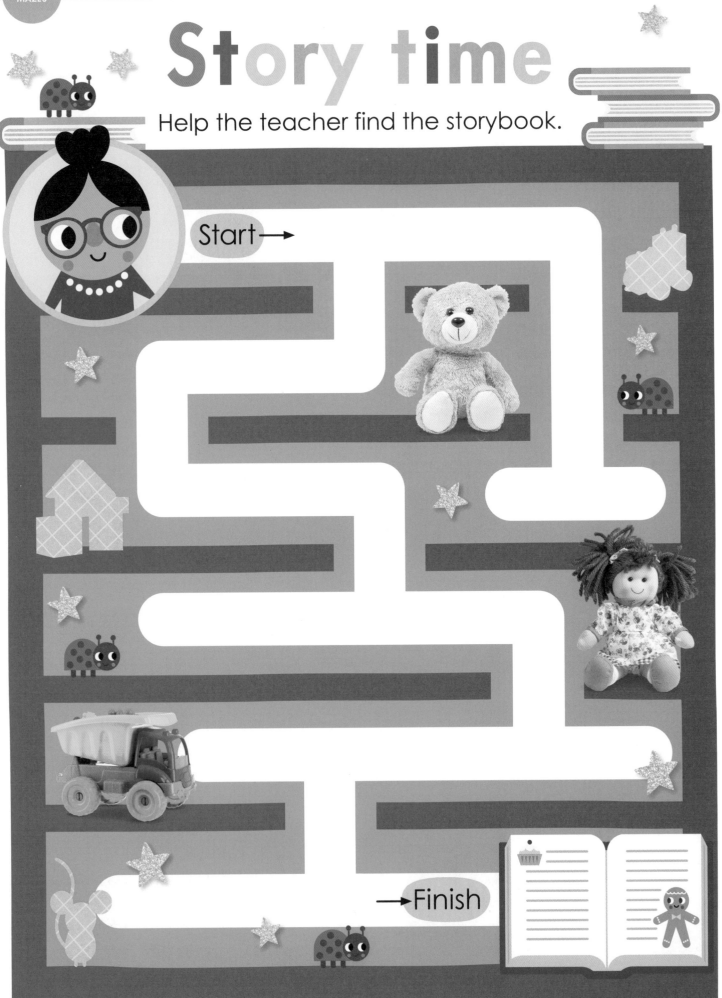

Start→

→Finish

Monster maze

Help the hero catch the monster.

Start →

→ Finish

Flower power

Help the bee fly around the flower.

Start

Finish

Playtime

Help the children find the toy box.

Start

Toys

Finish

Fly away home

Help the owl reach her owlets.

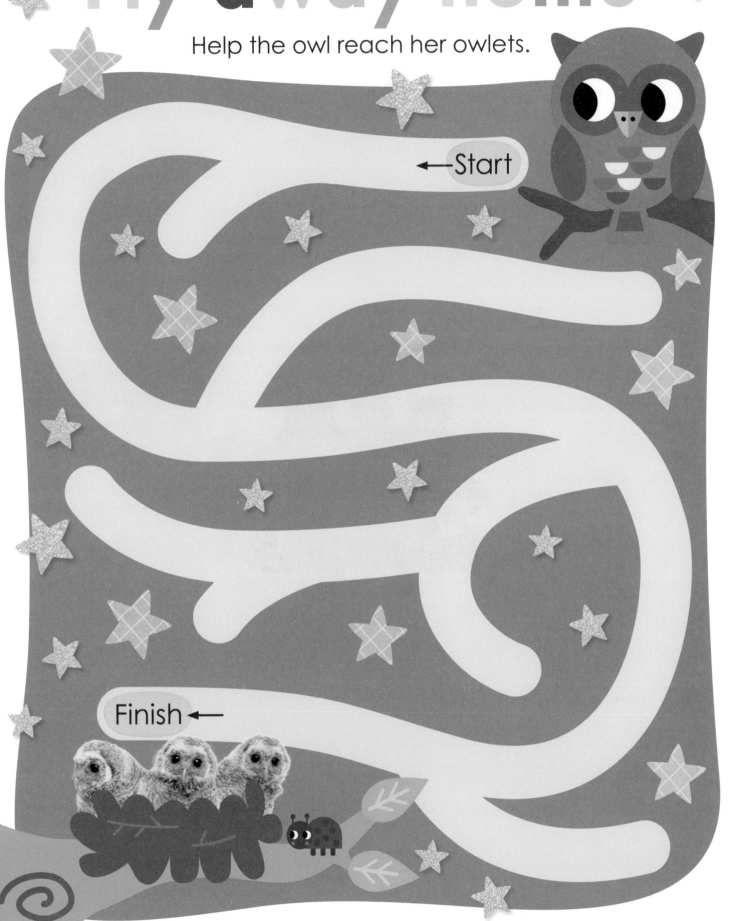

Start

Finish

Tiger tangle

Find your way through the tiger's stripes.

Start →

→ Finish

Red

Trace these **red** things.

STOP

Color these things **red**.

Green

Trace these **green** things.

Color these things **green**.

Blue

Trace these **blue** things.

Color these things **blue**.

Orange

Trace these **orange** things.

Color these things **orange**.

Yellow

Trace these **yellow** things.

Color these things **yellow**.

Purple

Trace these **purple** things.

Color these things **purple**.

Pink

Trace these **pink** things.

Color these things **pink**.

Brown

Trace these **brown** things.

Color these things **brown**.

Black

Trace these **black** things.

Color these things **black**.

White

Trace these **white** things.

Trace these white things.

Squares

Trace the **squares**.

Color Lily's square **blue**.

Trace and color
your square in **red**.

Rectangles

Trace the **rectangles**.

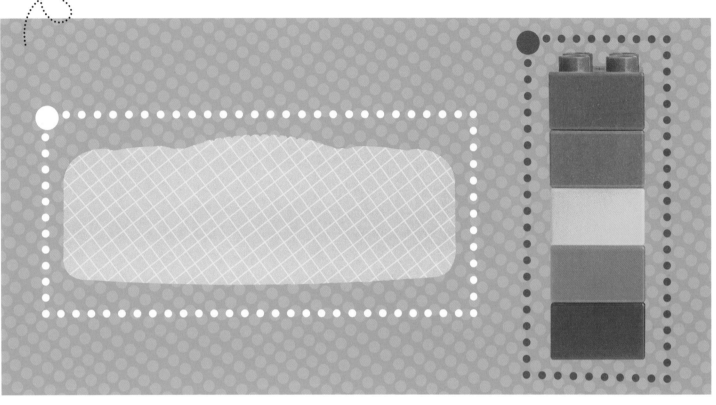

Color Jack's rectangle **green**.

Trace and color your rectangle in **yellow**.

Triangles

Trace the **triangles**.

Color Noah's triangle **orange**.

Trace and color your triangle in **purple**.

Circles

Trace the **circles**.

Color Ava's circle **pink**.

Trace and color
your circle in **brown**.

Ovals

Trace the **ovals**.

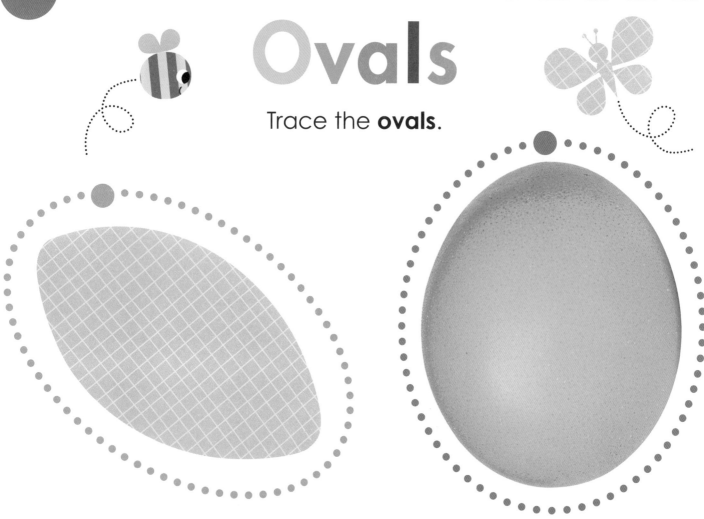

Color Abby's oval **orange**.

Trace and color
your oval in **blue**.

Stars

Trace the **stars**.

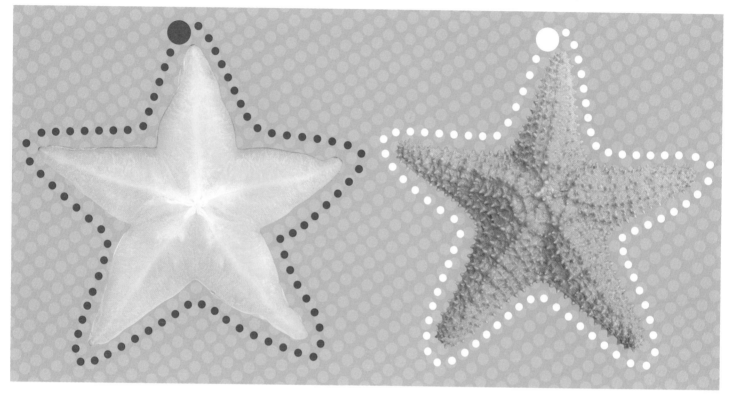

Color Ben's star **yellow**.

Trace and color
your star in **green**.

Hearts

Trace the **hearts**.

Color Luke's heart **pink**.

Trace and color
your heart in **red**.

Arrows

Trace the **arrows**.

Color Olivia's arrow green.

Trace and color
your arrow in pink.

FIRST
CONCEPTS

Match the shapes

Draw lines to match the shapes that are the same.

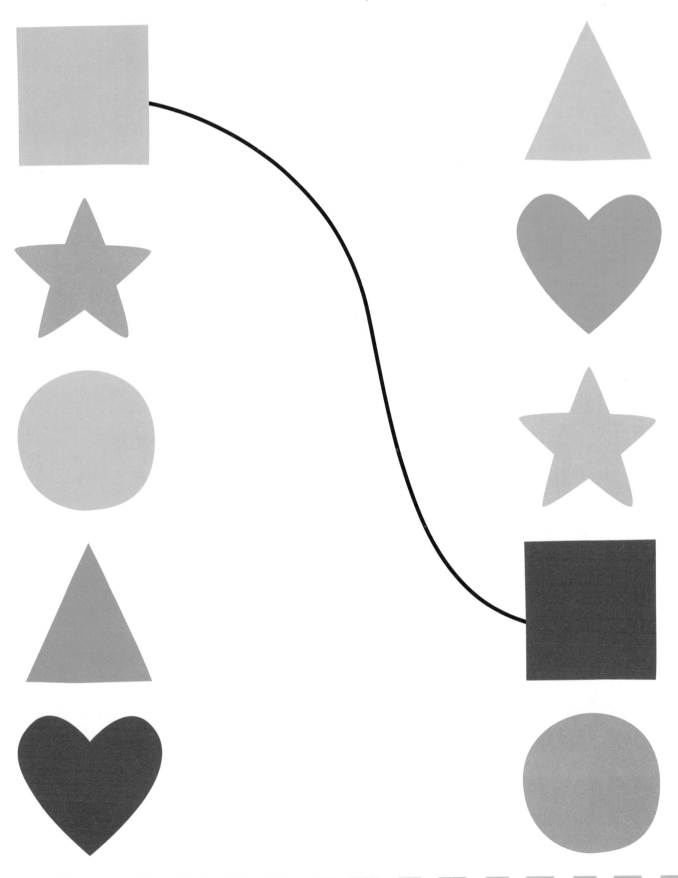

Match the objects

Draw lines to match the things that are the same shape.

Color the **A**.   Trace the letters with your finger.

astron**a**ut

Trace the dotted letters with your pencil.

Trace the uppercase and lowercase **a**'s.

Andy   apple

Color the B. **Trace the letters with your finger.**

banana

Trace the dotted letters with your pencil.

B B B B b b b b

Trace the uppercase and lowercase b's.

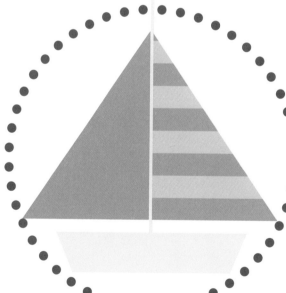

Belle   boat

Color the **C**.

Trace the letters with your finger.

cake

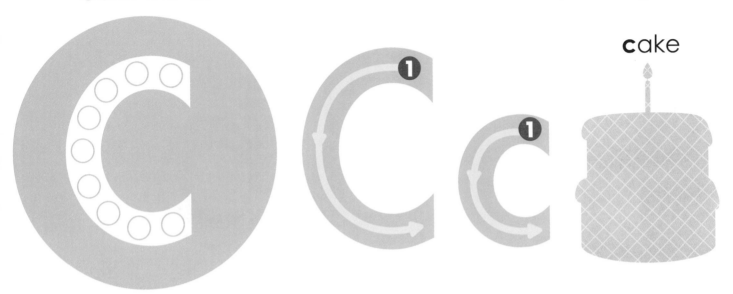

Trace the dotted letters with your pencil.

C C C c c c

Trace the uppercase and lowercase **c**'s.

Clara cat

Color the **D**.   Trace the letters with your finger.

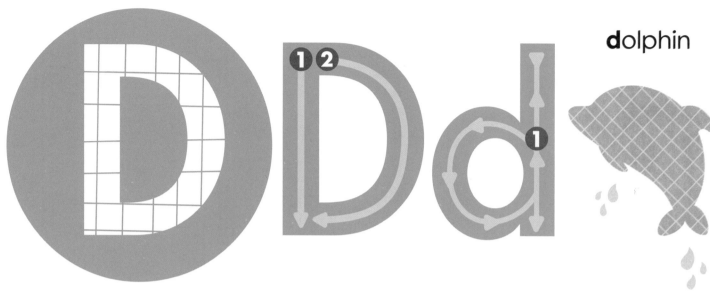

dolphin

Trace the dotted letters with your pencil.

Trace the uppercase and lowercase **d**'s.

Dylan   doll

Color the **E**.   Trace the letters with your finger.

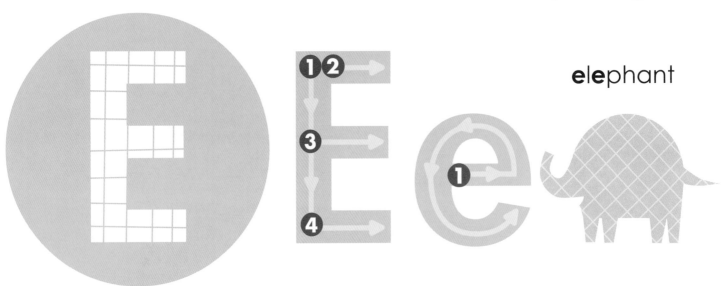

elephant

Trace the dotted letters with your pencil.

Trace the uppercase and lowercase **e**'s.

Eddie engine

Color the **F**.   Trace the letters with your finger.

fish

Trace the dotted letters with your pencil.

Trace the uppercase and lowercase **f**'s.

Fay   frog

Color the **G**.   Trace the letters with your finger.

grapes

Trace the dotted letters with your pencil.

Trace the uppercase and lowercase **g**'s.

Grace   goat

Color the **H**.   Trace the letters with your finger.

house

Trace the dotted letters with your pencil.

Trace the uppercase and lowercase **h**'s.

Henry   horse

Color the **I**.

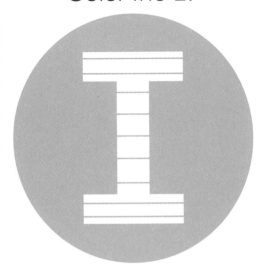

Trace the letters with your finger.

insect

Trace the dotted letters.

Ivy

Color the **J**.

Trace the letters with your finger.

jar

Trace the dotted letters.

Joe

Color the **K**.   Trace the letters with your finger.

koala

Trace the dotted letters with your pencil.

Trace the uppercase and lowercase **k**'s.

Kyle   kite

Color the **L**.

Trace the letters with your finger.

lamp

Trace the dotted letters with your pencil.

Trace the uppercase and lowercase **l**'s.

Luke   lemon

Color the **M**. Trace the letters with your finger.

mouse

Trace the dotted letters.

Mia

Color the **N**. Trace the letters with your finger.

nest

Trace the dotted letters.

Noah

Color the **O**.   Trace the letters with your finger.

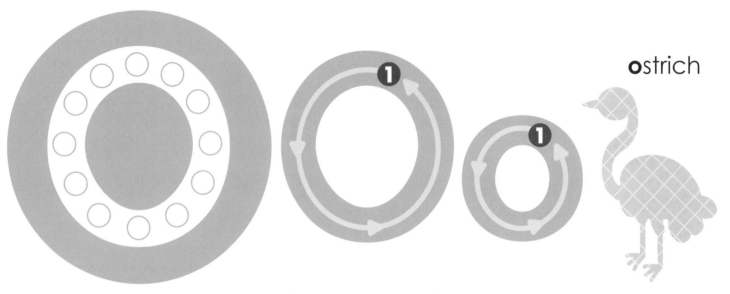

ostrich

Trace the dotted letters with your pencil.

Trace the uppercase and lowercase **o**'s.

Oliver   otter

Color the **P**.

Trace the letters with your finger.

pum**p**kin

Trace the dotted letters with your pencil.

P P P P p p p

Trace the uppercase and lowercase **p**'s.

Piper panda

Color the **Q**.

Trace the letters with your finger.

queen

Trace the dotted letters.

Quinn

Color the **R**.

Trace the letters with your finger.

ring

Trace the dotted letters.

Rose

Color the **S**.

Trace the letters with your finger.

snake

Trace the dotted letters with your pencil.

Trace the uppercase and lowercase **s**'s.

Simon   scarf

Color the **T**.

Trace the letters with your finger.

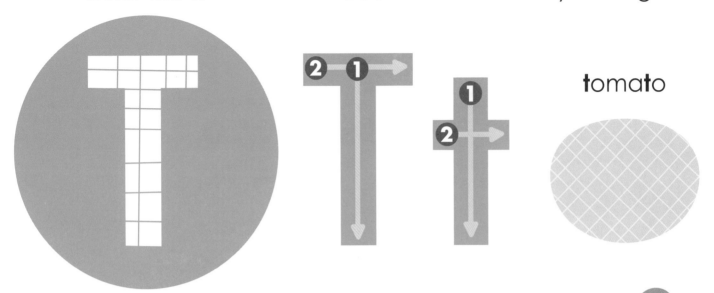

tomato

Trace the dotted letters with your pencil.

Trace the uppercase and lowercase **t**'s.

Tim

tiger

Color the **U**.   Trace the letters with your finger.

umbrella

Trace the dotted letters with your pencil.

Trace the uppercase and lowercase **u**'s.

Una

up

Color the **V**.

Trace the letters with your finger.

vet

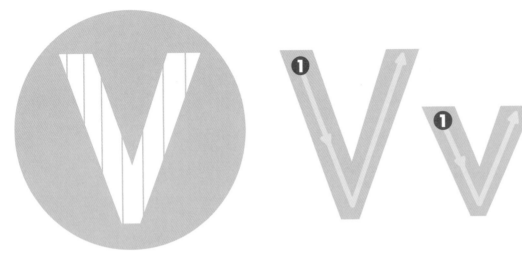

Trace the dotted letters.

V v

Vicky

Color the **W**.

Trace the letters with your finger.

wasp

Trace the dotted letters.

W w

Will

Color the **X**.

Trace the letters with your finger.

X-ray

Trace the dotted letters.

Xena

Color the **Y**.

Trace the letters with your finger.

yo-**y**o

Trace the dotted letters.

Yosef

Color the **Z**.

Trace the letters with your finger.

zebra

Trace the dotted letters.

Z Z Z Z z z z z

Trace the uppercase and lowercase **z**'s.

Zara   zero

Read the uppercase and lowercase alphabet.
Then trace the letters.

Aa Bb Cc Dd

Ee Ff Gg Hh

Ii Jj Kk Ll Mm

Nn Oo Pp Qq

Rr Ss Tt Uu Vv

Ww Xx Yy Zz

Snake starts with s

Say the words. What sound do they start with?

 snake   **ski**   **sing**

Circle the words that start with the **s** sound.

 (swan)

sign   **bus**

Teddy starts with t

Say the words. What sound do they start with?

turkey top teddy

Draw lines from the **t** to the words that start with **t**.

 tiger

 towel

ball table

85

Panda starts with p

Say the words. What sound do they start with?

panda   pie   pirate

Say the words aloud and circle the **p**'s.

 puppet   puppy

86

Nest starts with n

Say the words. What sound do they start with?

nest   **nurse**   **nine**

Check the words that begin with **n**.

 nuts

 nose

✔

 socks

 net

Mouse starts with m

Say the words. What sound do they start with?

mouse   map mittens

Circle the words that start with the **m** sound.

mug

hat monkey

Doll starts with d

Say the words. What sound do they start with?

doll　　　duck　　　dog

Draw lines from the **d** to the words that start with **d**.

dive

turtle

d

dice

deer

Goat starts with g

Say the words. What sound do they start with?

goat   grapes   gift

Say the words aloud and circle the **g**'s.

goggles   giggle

Robot starts with r

Say the words. What sound do they start with?

robot   rat   rabbit

Check the words that begin with **r**.

 rhino   radio

 rope   train

Car starts with c

Say the words. What sound do they start with?

car   coat   carrot

Circle the words that start with the **c** sound.

cow

comb

fish

92

Kitten starts with k

Say the words. What sound do they start with?

kitten   **key**   **king**

Draw lines from the **k** to the words that start with **k**.

 tent

 kiss

 k

 koala

 kite

Bus starts with b

Say the words. What sound do they start with?

bus   bird   bee

Say the words aloud and circle the **b**'s.

bib   bubble

Hippo starts with h

Say the words. What sound do they start with?

hippo **hen** **honey**

Check the words that begin with **h**.

 house

 frog

 hat

 horse

95

Fish starts with f

Say the words. What sound do they start with?

fish   fork   fox

Circle the words that start with the **f** sound.

fairy   tree   feather

Jump starts with j

Say the words. What sound do they start with?

jump   jar jigsaw

Draw lines from the **j** to the words that start with **j**.

jacket   **j**   jewels

juice   insect

Leaf starts with l

Say the words. What sound do they start with?

leaf   lamb   lime

Say the words aloud and circle the l's.

lily   lollipop

Vet starts with v

Say the words. What sound do they start with?

vet **vest** **vase**

Check the words that begin with **v**.

crab

violet

☐

☐

violin

van

☐

☐

Watch starts with w

Say the words. What sound do they start with?

watch   web   wagon

Circle the words that start with the **w** sound.

snail

worm

wig

Yo-yo starts with y

Say the words. What sound do they start with?

yo-yo yak yawn

Draw lines from the **y** to the words that start with **y**.

truck

y

yell

yellow yogurt

Quiet starts with q

Say the words. What sound do they start with?

quiet   queen   quail

Circle the words that start with the **q** sound.

Quack!

quack   bear   quilt

Fox ends with x

Say the words. What sound do they end with?

fox   six   box

Check the words that have an **x** in them.

mix

ox

taxi

sock

103

Zebra starts with z

Say the words. What sound do they start with?

zebra   zero   zoo

Say the words aloud and circle the **z**'s.

Buzz!
Buzz!

zigzag   buzz

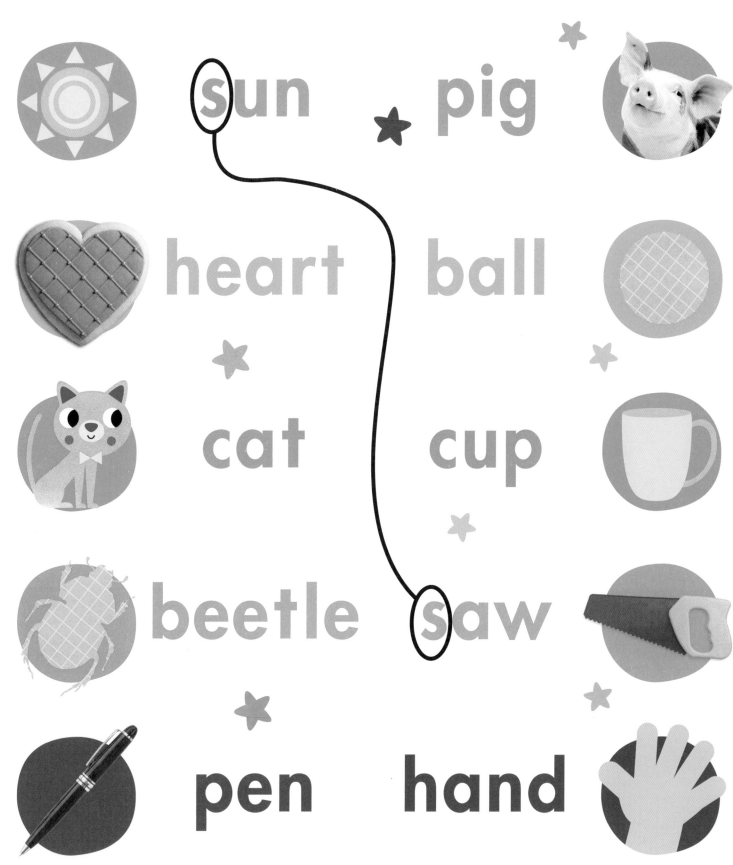

Match the sounds

Draw lines to match the words that start with the same sound.

sun

pig

heart

ball

cat

cup

beetle

saw

pen

hand

Match the rhymes

Say the words. Draw lines to match the rhymes.

cat

dog

frog

bat

Circle the rhyme

Circle the word that rhymes.

mouse

house   **cup**

car

snake   **star**

Match the rhymes

Draw lines to match the rhymes.

hen

dice

ice

pen

Circle the rhyme

Circle the word that rhymes.

sock

clock   cake

duck

truck   ball

Connect the rhymes

Draw lines from the **pug** to the things that rhyme with it.

mug

pie

pug

rug

hug

Find the rhymes

Circle the words that rhyme with **wing**.

ring

hat

fish

king

sing

string

koala

Connect the rhymes

Draw lines from the **skate** to the things that rhyme with it.

eight

gate

skate

cat

plate

Find the rhymes

Circle the words that rhyme with **nail**.

whale

teddy

plane

tail

moon

snail

Match the rhymes

Draw lines to match the rhymes.

snake

cake

man

can

Circle the rhyme

Circle the word that rhymes.

chick

rocket brick

shark

park flower

What's wrong?

Circle the word that doesn't rhyme.

bun **baby** **run**

pot **hop** **mop**

Rhyming words

Trace the rhymes.

10

ten

pen

pig

dig

What's wrong?

Circle the word that doesn't rhyme.

cat　　**cap**　　**clap**

call　　**ball**　　**bell**

Rhyming words

Trace the rhymes.

top

pop

dad

sad

Match the rhymes

Draw lines to match the rhymes.

jet

honey

vet

shark

money

Woof!

bark

Rhyming words

Trace the rhymes.

hat

rat

hit

knit

Match the rhymes

Draw lines to match the rhymes.

ham

jam

skip

pan

van

sip

Rhyming words

Trace the rhymes.

Circle the rhyme

Circle the word that rhymes.

jeans

carrots beans

talk

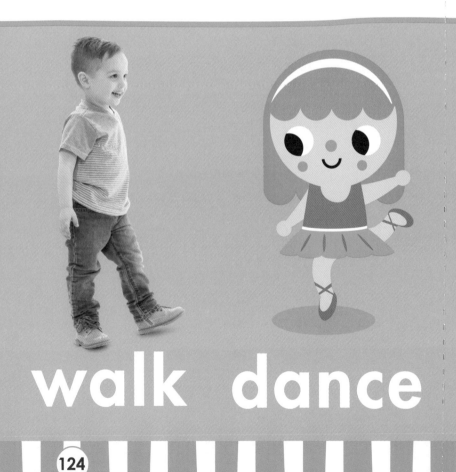

walk dance

Rhyming words

Trace the rhymes.

snap! snap!

snap

cap

moon

spoon

fork

stork

Trace the letters with your finger.

athlete

Trace the letters with your pencil.

ant

Trace the letters with your finger.

bike

Trace the letters with your pencil.

bee

Trace the letters with your finger.

car

Trace the letters with your pencil.

cake

Trace the letters with your finger.

duck

Trace the letters with your pencil.

doll

Trace the letters with your finger.

E e engine

Trace the letters with your pencil.

E E E E E

e e e e e

elf

Trace the letters with your finger.

1 2 → **1**
3 → **2**

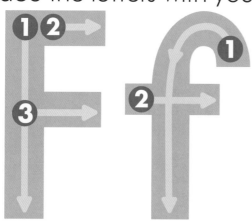

fairy

Trace the letters with your pencil.

F F F F F

f f f f f

frog

Trace the letters with your finger.

G g g

gloves

Trace the letters with your pencil.

G G G G

g g g g

goat

Trace the letters with your finger.

house

Trace the letters with your pencil.

H H H H H

h h h h h

hen

Trace the letters with your finger and then with your pencil.

ice

jet

Trace the letters with your finger.

 key

Trace the letters with your pencil.

kite

Trace the letters with your finger.

lizard

Trace the letters with your pencil.

lamp

Trace the letters with your finger.

monster

Trace the letters with your pencil.

mouse

Trace the letters with your finger.

nest

Trace the letters with your pencil.

 N N N N

n n n n n

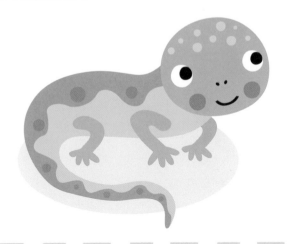

n **ewt**

Trace the letters with your finger.

ostrich

Trace the letters with your pencil.

orange

Trace the letters with your finger.

parrot

Trace the letters with your pencil.

P P P P P

p p p p p

puppy

Trace the letters with your finger and then with your pencil.

queen

rabbit

Trace the letters with your finger.

spider

Trace the letters with your pencil.

 snake

Trace the letters with your finger.

tiger

Trace the letters with your pencil.

tent

Trace the letters with your finger.

1 U **1** u

umbrella

Trace the letters with your pencil.

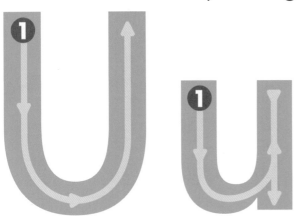

U U U U

u u u u u u

up

Trace the letters with your finger and then with your pencil.

van

wolf

Trace the letters with your finger and then with your pencil.

X-ray

yo-yo

Trace the letters with your finger.

1 Z **1** z

zigzag

Trace the letters with your pencil.

Z Z Z Z Z

z z z z z

zebra

Color the **1**. Then count **1** pig.

one

Trace **1** bow.

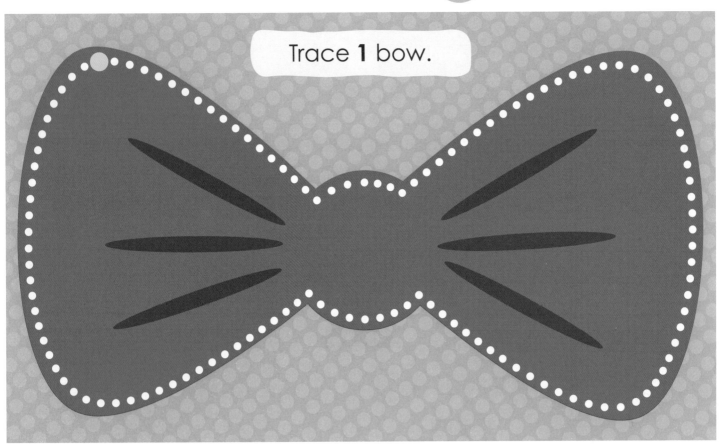

Trace the **1**'s with your finger and then with your pencil.

Color **1** car.

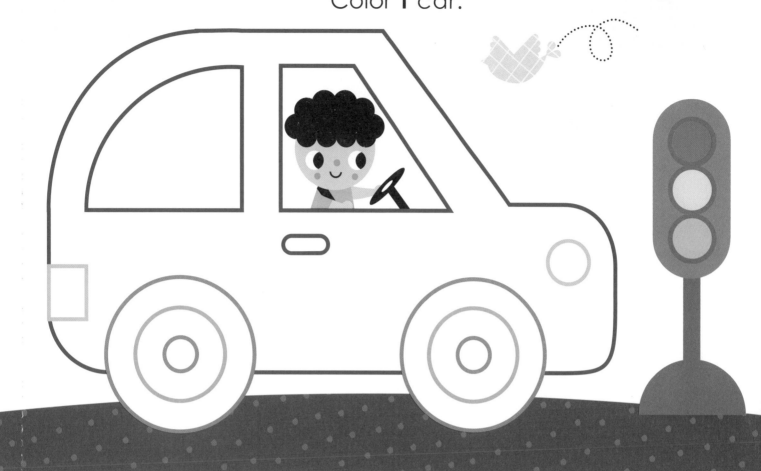

Circle the plate with **1** cupcake on it.

2
two

Color the **2**. Then count **2** gloves.

① ②

Trace **2** shirts.

Trace the **2**'s with your finger and then with your pencil.

① 2 2 2 2 2 2

Count and color **2** butterflies.

Circle the ladybug that has **2** spots.

3
three

Color the **3**. Then count **3** strawberries.

1 2 3

Trace **3** kites.

Trace the **3**'s with your finger and then with your pencil.

① 3 3 3 3 3 3

Color **3** fish.

Add **3** stickers to finish the **3** flowers.

Count the cats.

153

4

four

Color the **4**. Then count **4** trucks.

1

2

3

4

Trace **4** stars.

Trace the **4**'s with your finger and then with your pencil.

4 4 4 4 4 4

Circle the jar with **4** candies.

Color and sticker **4** beach balls.

Count the mice.

5
five

Color the **5**. Then count **5** frogs.

Trace **5** bananas.

Trace the **5**'s with your finger and then with your pencil.

5 5 5 5 5 5 5

Count the objects in each group.
Then draw lines to match the groups to the numbers.

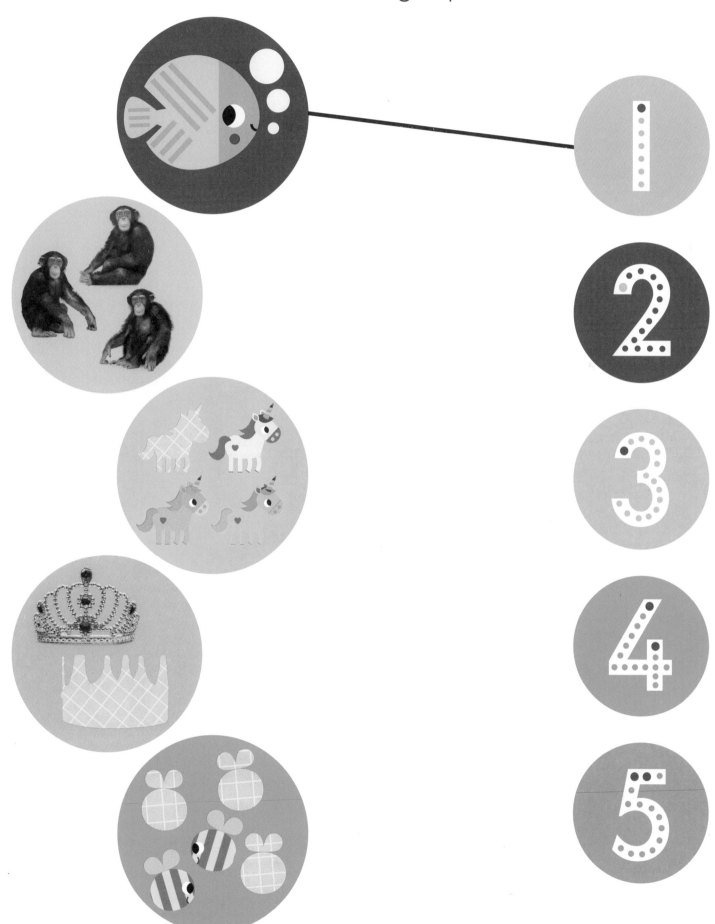

Color the **6**. Then count **6** hats.

6

six

1 2 3

4 5 6

Trace **6** buttons.

Trace the **6**'s with your finger and then with your pencil.

Follow the **6**'s to guide the rabbit to its burrow.

Start → 6 6 6

4

6

5

5 5 4

5 5

5

6 6 6

6

5

3 6 6 2

3 6 2 2

3 6

3 6 6 → Finish

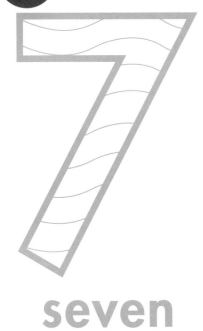

seven

Color the **7**. Then count **7** chicks.

Trace **7** shells.

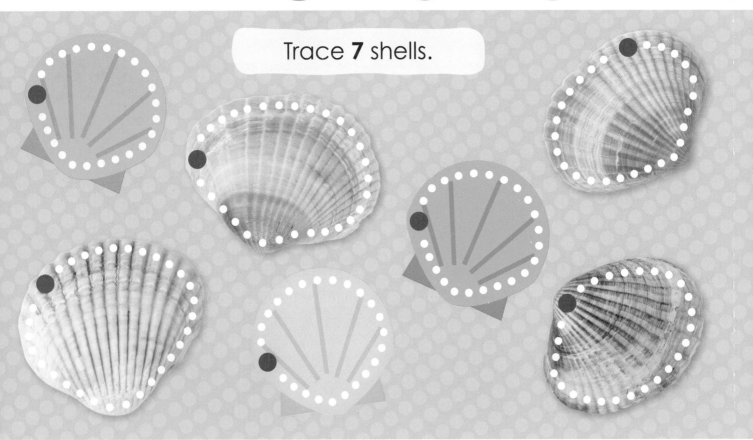

Trace the **7**'s with your finger and then with your pencil.

Circle the tiger with **7** stripes.

Count and color **7** pieces of fruit.

Color the **8**. Then count **8** birds.

8

eight

1 2 3 4

5 6 7 8

Trace **8** yo-yos.

Trace the **8**'s with your finger and then with your pencil.

Count the animals in the zoo.

Add stickers to finish the **8** lollipops.

Color **8** spots on the dog.

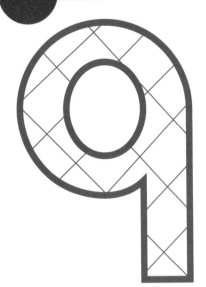

nine

Color the **9**. Then count **9** jewels.

Trace **9** leaves.

Trace the **9**'s with your finger and then with your pencil.

Color **9** gifts.

Trace **9** spikes on the dinosaur's back.

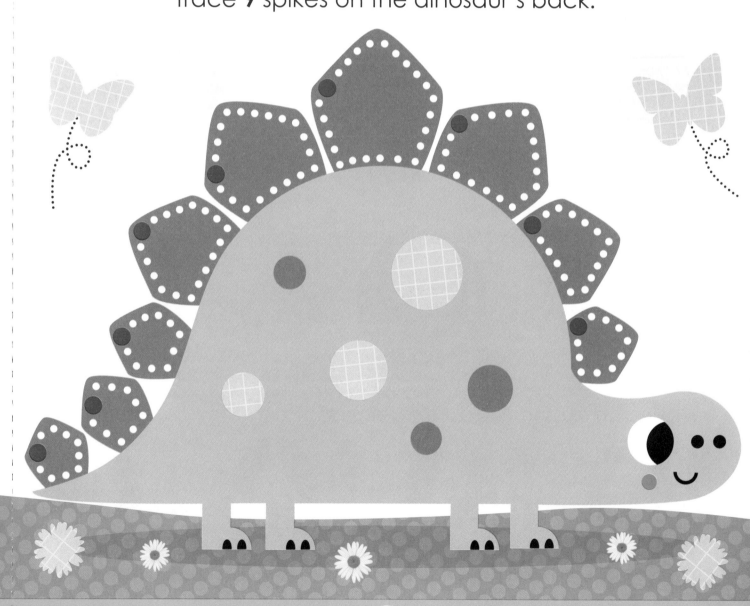

10

ten

Color the **10**. Then count **10** socks.

1 2 3 4 5

6 7 8 9 10

Trace **10** cookies.

Trace the **10**'s with your finger and then with your pencil.

10 10 10 10

Count the objects in each group.
Then draw lines to match the groups to the numbers.

What's different?

Circle the picture that is different.

Circle the picture that is different.

What's different?

Circle the picture that is different.

Circle the picture that is different.

What's different?

Circle the bear that is different.

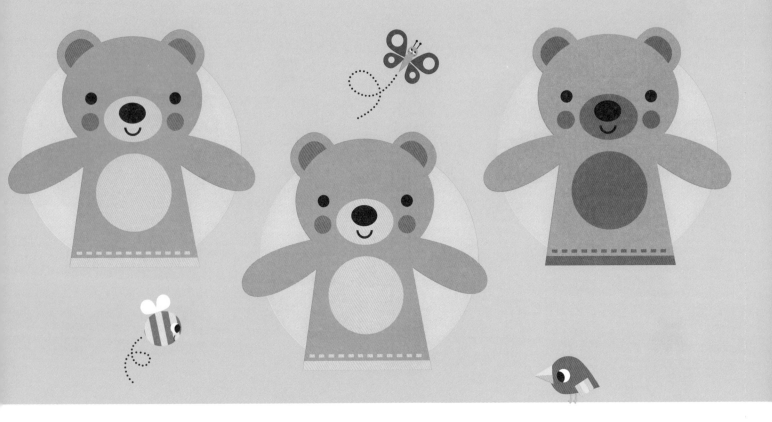

Circle the tricycle that is different.

What's different?

Circle the puppy that is different.

Circle the flower that is different.

Make them different

Give the **yellow** emoji a happy smile.
Give the **blue** emoji a sad mouth.

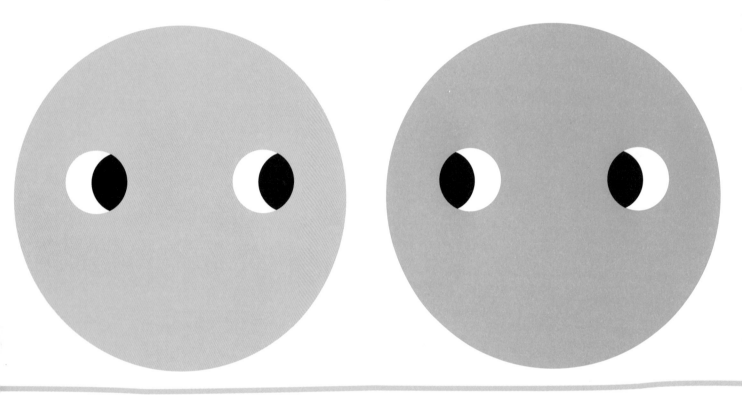

Color the buses different colors.

Make them different

Give one dinosaur **red** spots.
Give the other dinosaur **blue** spots.

Color the girls' clothes different colors.

Looking the same

Circle the rabbits that are the same.

Color the other tractor the same colors as this one.

Find the pair

Circle the button that is the same as this one.

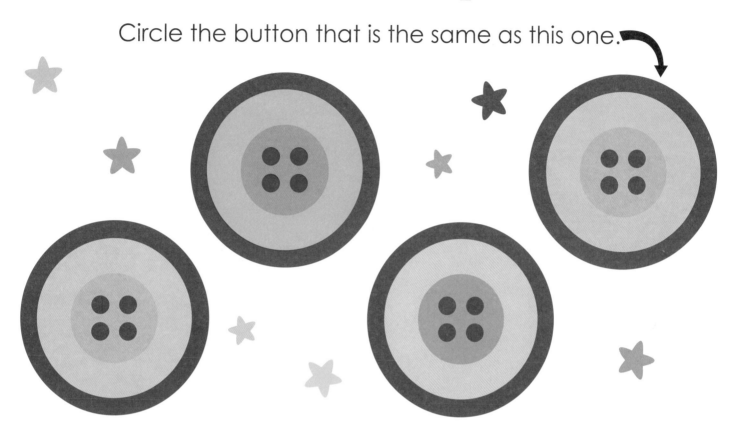

Circle the shell that is the same as this one.

Match the pairs

Draw lines to join the pictures that are the same.

Match the pairs

Draw lines to join the pictures that are the same.

Put them away

Draw a line from each building brick
to the box with its matching color.

red   green   blue

Put them away

Draw lines from the knives, forks, and spoons to the correct trays.

Match the size

Circle the cone with the same amount of ice cream as this one.

Circle the tree that is the same size as this one.

Match the height

Circle the boy who is the same height as this one.

Circle the giraffe that is the same height as this one.

Find the biggest

Circle the biggest bunch of flowers.

Circle the tallest girl.

Find the smallest

Circle the smaliest butterfly.

Circle the shortest dog.

Find the difference

Circle the monkey that is upside down.

Circle the picture that is upside down.

Find the difference

Circle the child who is facing the other way from the others.

Circle the fish that is facing the other way from the others.

Animals grow

Look at the growing kitten.
Circle the picture where he is the youngest.

What comes first? Sticker the numbers 1 to 3 in order.

Plants grow

Look at the growing plant.
Circle the picture where it is the oldest.

What comes first? Sticker the numbers 1 to 3 in order.

Plants we eat

Much of the food we eat comes from plants.
Draw lines to match the plant with the food.

What animals eat

Some animals eat plants and some eat meat.
Draw lines from the animals to the things they eat.

Fur, feathers, and scales

Sticker the rabbit with the other furry animals.

Sticker the snake with the other scaly animals.

Sticker the parrot with the other feathered animals.

Animal homes

Draw lines to match the animals with their homes.

Leaf shapes

Different trees have differently shaped leaves.
Draw lines to match the leaves.

pine needles

oak leaf

holly leaf

maple leaf

Pretty flowers

Draw lines to match the flowers.
Color the flowers on the right to match the ones on the left.

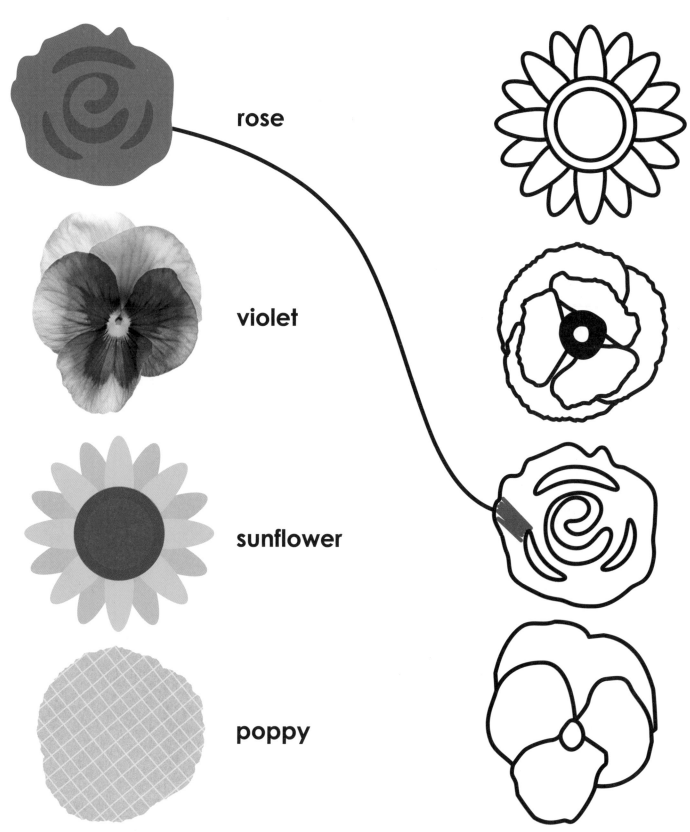

rose

violet

sunflower

poppy

Day and night

Sticker the animals we see during the day in the daytime scene.

Sticker the animals we see at night in the nighttime scene.

Shadows

Shadows form in places where light cannot reach.
Draw lines to match the animals with their shadows.

Seasons

Sticker the correct season name into each scene.

A tree through the year

Trees change with the seasons.

Sticker **blossoms** on the spring tree.

Sticker **apples** on the summer tree.

Sticker a **snowman** under the winter tree.

Sticker **colorful leaves** on the fall tree.

VERY FIRST SCIENCE

Weather

Trace the raindrops in the rainy scene.

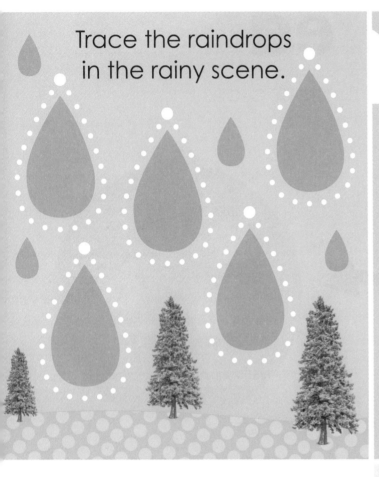

Trace the sun's rays in the sunny scene.

Trace the snowflakes in the snowy scene.

Trace the wind's path in the windy scene.

Rainbows

Rainbows form when the sun shines through raindrops.
Color the rainbow's stripes the same colors as the dots.

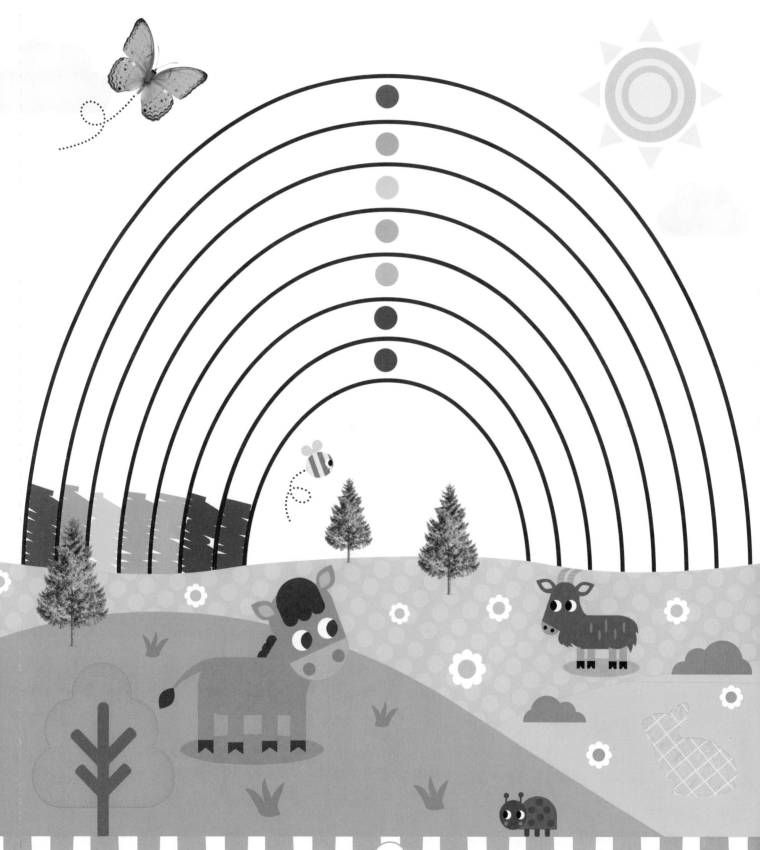

Heavy or light?

Sticker a brick by the things that are heavy.
Sticker a feather by the things that are light.

Fast or slow?

Some things move fast. Some things move slowly.
Circle the things that move fast.

Push or pull?

Circle the things we push with a **blue** pencil.
Circle the things we pull with a **red** pencil.

Is it stretchy?

Some things stretch when we pull them. Other things do not.
Circle the stretchy things.

Jobs people do

Name the jobs. Then circle all the ones that you'd like to do.

doctor

teacher

barber

letter carrier

farmer

baker

storekeeper

mechanic

To the rescue!

Draw lines to connect the emergency workers with their jobs.

police officer

helping sick people

firefighter

helping lost children

paramedic

firefighting

On the road

Name the vehicles.
Then circle the ones you've seen on roads near you.

car

taxi

unicycle

bicycle

bus

truck

motorcycle

digger

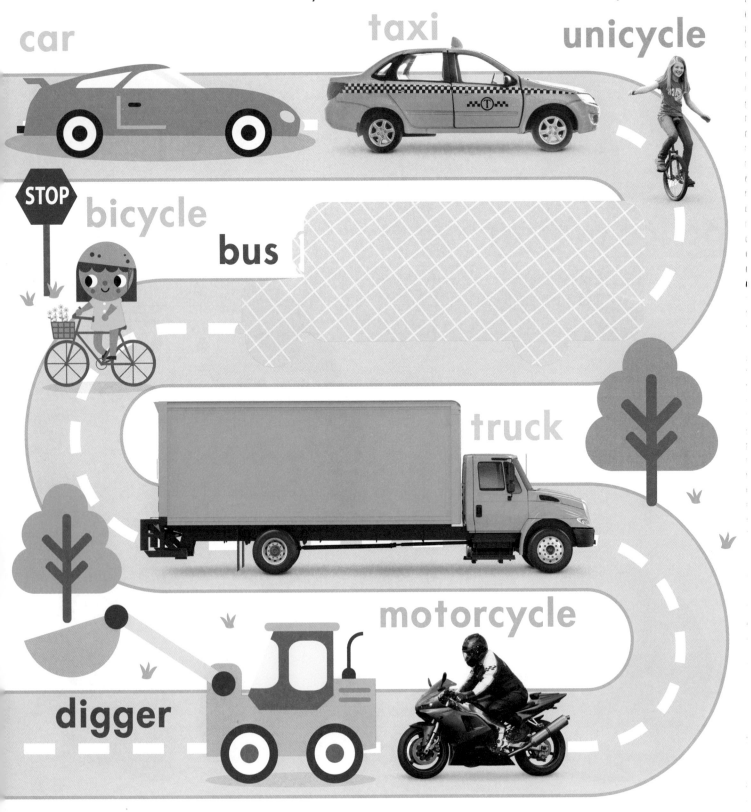

In the sky

Name the vehicles.
Then circle the ones you've seen in the sky above you.

hot-air balloon

airplane

rocket

parachute

hang glider

helicopter

In the city

Cross out the things that don't belong in the city.

In the country

Cross out the things that don't belong in the country.

In the forest

Find, name, and circle all the animals in this forest scene.

In the ocean

Find, name, and circle all the sea creatures in this ocean scene.

Keeping fit

Draw lines to join the equipment with the activity.

soccer ball

swimming

water wings

biking

tricycle

playing soccer

Fun activities

Draw lines to join the equipment with the activity.

pencils

sliding

slide

reading

book

drawing

Going shopping

Draw lines to join the objects with the stores where we buy them.

shoes   **teddy bear**   **dog bed**

Toy Store

Pet Store

Shoe Store

At the supermarket

Name the foods. Then circle the ones that your family buys.

eggs

MILK

milk

yogurt

cereal

apples

corn

carrots

sausages

Keeping safe

Circle the things that help keep you safe.
Cross out the things that are dangerous.

running with
scissors

wearing
a seatbelt

wearing a
bike helmet

playing with
matches

Crossing the road

Circle the things that help keep you safe.
Cross out the things that are dangerous.

looking both ways

using a crosswalk

crossing with
an adult

running into
the road

Who can help?

Circle the people who you can ask for help.

a baby

parents

a police officer

a teacher

A is for apple.

All about me

If I get lost, I can tell people who I am.

My name is

....

My phone number is

....

I live at

....

....

More about me

Circle all the things that describe you.

I am a girl.

I have curly hair.

I am a boy.

I like trucks.

I like animals.

I have straight hair.

My picture

Here are some children. Draw yourself with the children.

Time for preschool

Let's go to preschool!
Circle the things you say when you get to preschool.
Cross out the things that would be silly to say.

At preschool

At preschool, you might have a cubby.
Color and sticker this cubby picture.

Draw lines from the cubby to the things that you can store in your cubby.

coat

cow

backpack

helmet

piano

boots

Playing inside

Sometimes you will play inside.
Circle the playtime activities.
Cross out the things you don't do at playtime.

sleeping

reading

dressing up

taking a bath

building

playing with trains

painting

doing a jigsaw puzzle

Story time

A teacher might read you a story.
Color and sticker this story-time picture.

What do you do when the teacher is reading?
Circle the correct picture.

talk to friends   **listen to the story**

How do you ask a question? Circle the correct picture.

put up your hand   **shut your eyes**

Snack time

Circle the things you might eat and drink at snack time.
Cross out the things you do not eat.

yogurt

bowl

hat

sandwich

apple

milk

chair

fruit juice

Nap time

At preschool, you might take a nap.
Sticker and color the nap-time picture.

Wash your hands

Draw lines from the girl washing her hands to the times when you should wash your hands.

after using the bathroom

after reading

before eating

after getting dirty

Making things

Match the things you use to make things
with the pictures of children using them.

glue stick

drawing

crayons

sticking

cutting out

modeling clay

molding

painting

paints

scissors

Making music

Match the musical instruments with the people using them.

drum

playing the recorder

recorder

playing a drum

piano

playing the xylophone

triangle

playing the triangle

xylophone

playing the piano

Home time

Circle the things you can take home from preschool.
Cross out the things you leave at preschool.

art

backpack

table

water bottle

coat

lunch box

teacher

Congratulations!

GOOD WORK AWARD!

Name: ....

has successfully completed the

Get Ready for
Pre-K
Jumbo Workbook

Date: ....

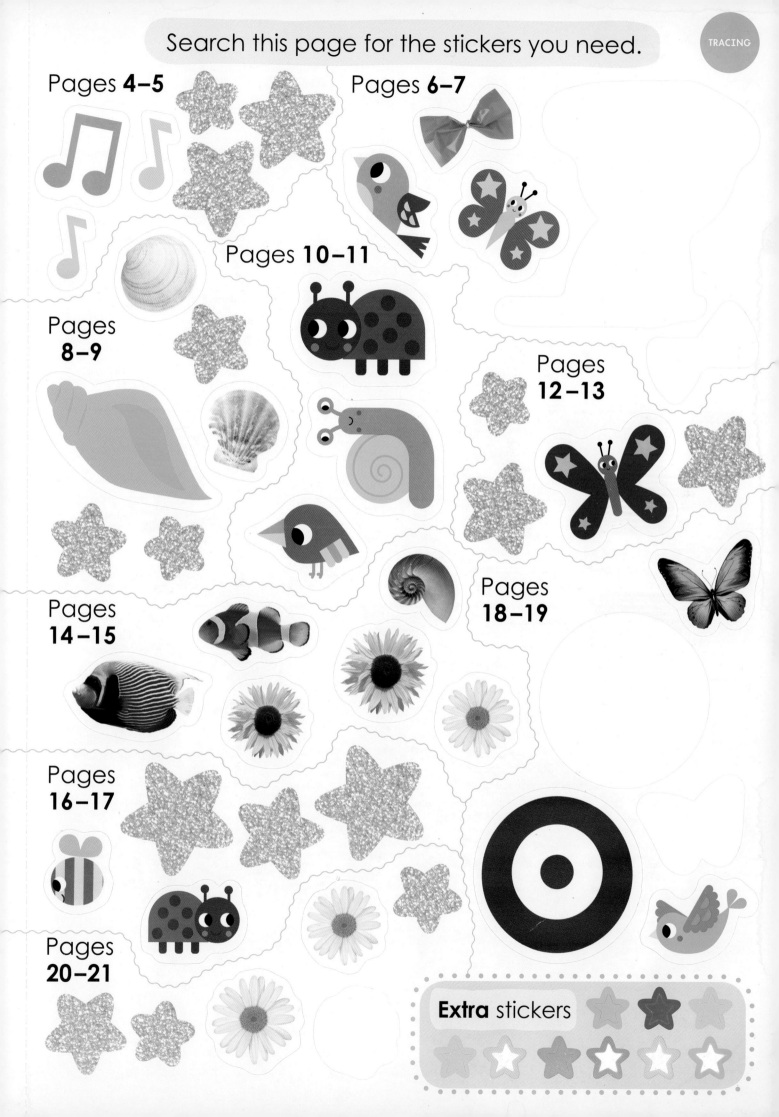

Search this page for the stickers you need.

TRACING

Pages **4–5**

Pages **6–7**

Pages **10–11**

Pages **8–9**

Pages **12–13**

Pages **14–15**

Pages **18–19**

Pages **16–17**

Pages **20–21**

Extra stickers

Search this page for the stickers you need.

FIRST MAZES

Pages
22–23

Pages **24–25**

Pages
26–27

Pages
28–29

Pages
30–31

Pages
32–33

Pages
34–35

Pages
38–39

Pages
36–37

Pages
40–41

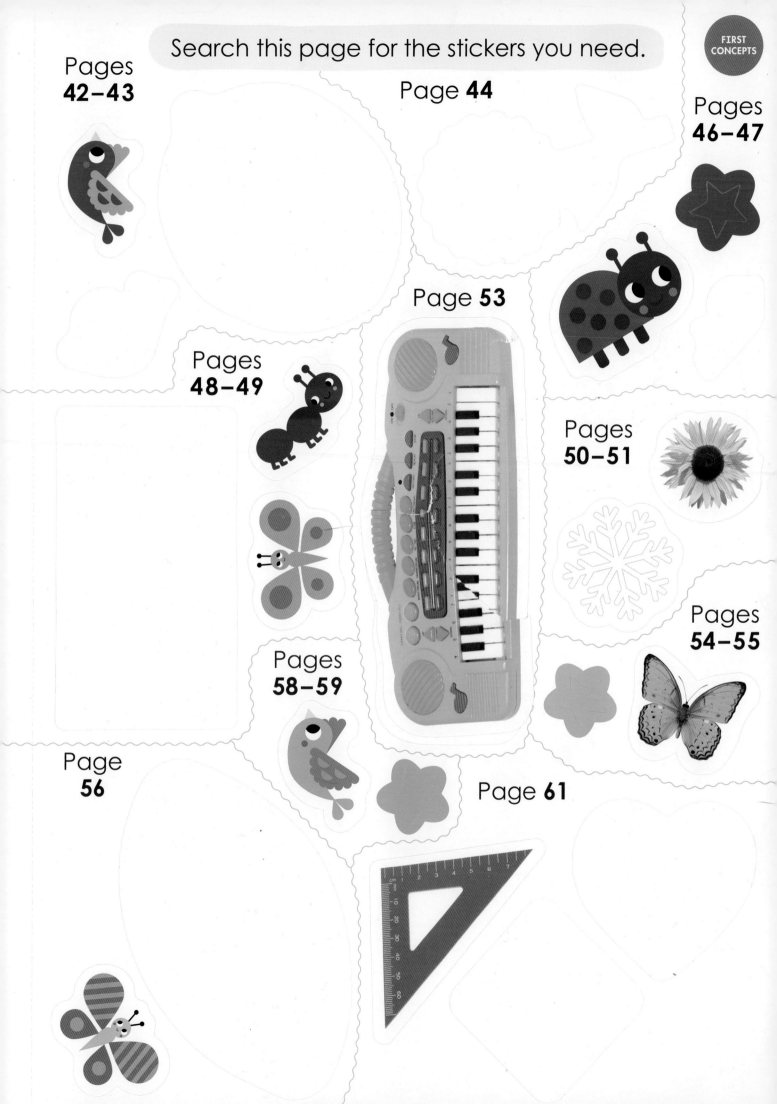

Search this page for the stickers you need.

Pages
42–43

Page 44

FIRST
CONCEPTS

Pages
46–47

Page 53

Pages
48–49

Pages
50–51

Pages
54–55

Pages
58–59

Page
56

Page 61

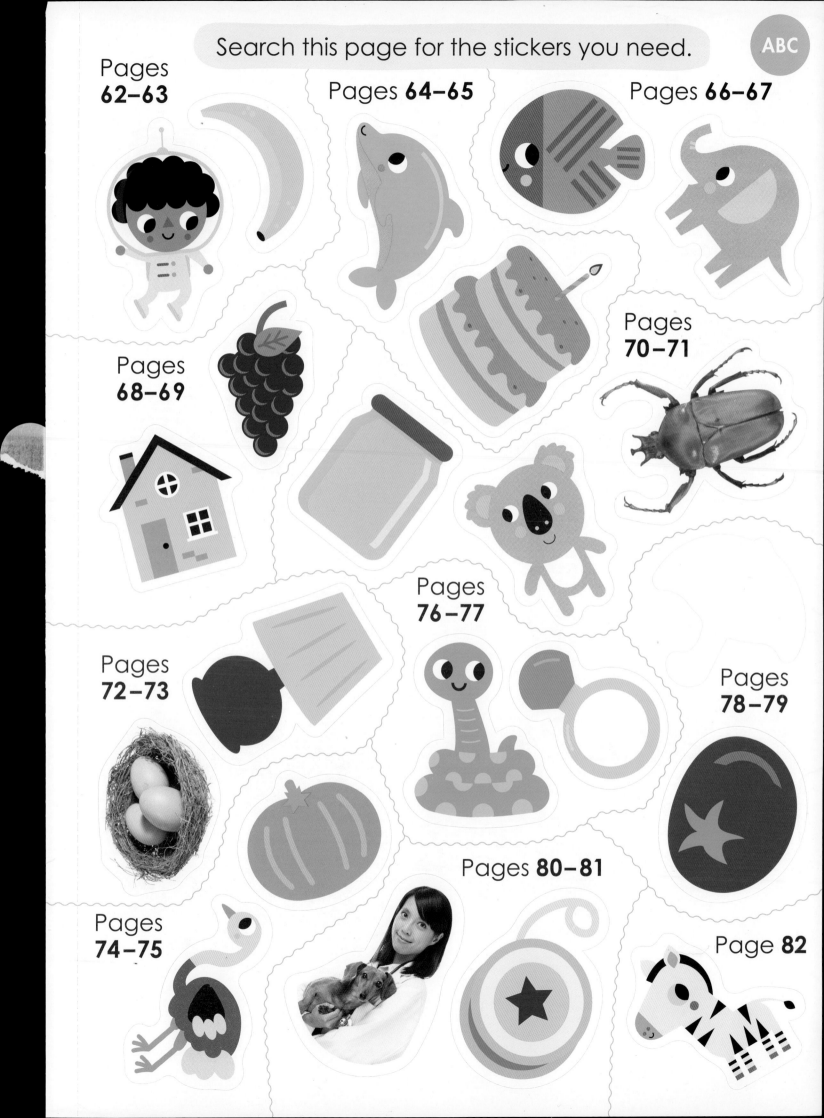

Search this page for the stickers you need.

Pages
62–63

Pages 64–65

Pages 66–67

Pages
70–71

Pages
68–69

Pages
76–77

Pages
72–73

Pages
78–79

Pages 80–81

Pages
74–75

Page 82

Search this page for the stickers you need.

FIRST LETTER SOUNDS

Pages **84–85**

Pages **86–87**

Pages **88–89**

Pages **90–91**

Pages **92–93**

Pages **94–95**

Pages **96–97**

Pages **98–99**

Pages **100–101**

Pages **102–103**

Pages **104–105**

Extra stickers

Search this page for the stickers you need.

RHYMES

Pages **106–107**

Pages **108–109**

Pages **110–111**

Pages **112–113**

Page **116**

Pages **114–115**

Page **118**

Page **120**

Pages **124–125**

Pages **122–123**

Extra stickers

Search this page for the stickers you need.

Pages 126–127

Page 129

Page 130

Page 133

Page 135

Page 136

Page 139

Pages 140–141

Page 142

Pages 144–145

Page 147

Extra stickers

Search this page for the stickers you need.

COUNTING

Page 149

Page 151

Page 153

Page 157

Page 155

Page 159

Page 165

Page 161

Page 163

Page 167

Extra stickers

Search this page for the stickers you need.

Pages **168–169**

Page **171**

Page **172**

Pages **174–175**

Pages **176–177**

Page **178**

Page **181**

Page **185**

Pages **182–183**

Extra stickers

Search this page for the stickers you need.

VERY FIRST SCIENCE

Pages
186–187

Page **190**

Pages
188–189

Page **193**

Page **194**

Pages
196–197

Page **199**

Page **200**

Pages
202–203

Extra stickers

Search this page for the stickers you need.

Pages **204–205**

Pages **206–207**

Pages
210–211

Pages
208–209

Pages
212–213

Pages **214–215**

Pages **216–217**

Page
219

Pages **220–221**

Extra stickers